1p @ 35.00

14.98
H
11/92

The Dragon Kingdom

ༀ། སྐྱེ་བཞིའི་དཔལ་ལ་ལྡན་འབྲུག་རྒྱལ་མཆོག་དང་སྐྱེ་ནེ་

ཆབ་འབངས་ཡོངས་ལ་ང་ཚོས་བཀྲ་ཤིས་བདེ་ལེགས་

ཞུ།

With gratitude for the hospitality of the royal family and the Bhutanese people.

Good fortune and blessings to all beings

The Dragon Kingdom

Images of Bhutan

Text by Blanche Christine Olschak

Translated from the German
by Michael H. Kohn

Photographs by
Ursula Markus-Gansser
and Augusto Gansser

Shambhala

Boston, Halifax & Shaftesbury

1988

Contents

SHAMBHALA PUBLICATIONS, INC.

Horticultural Hall
300 Massachusetts Avenue
Boston, Massachusetts 02115

The Foundry Building
858 Barrington Street
P.O. Box 1556
Halifax, N.S. B3J 2Y3

The Old School House
The Courtyard, Bell Street
Shaftesbury, Dorset SP7 8BP

© 1983 by Atlantis Verlag,
Freiburg im Breisgau
English translation © 1988
by Shambhala Publications, Inc.

All rights reserved. No part of this book may be reproduced in any form or by any means, electronic or mechanical, including photocopying, recording, or by an information storage and retrieval system, without permission in writing from the publisher.

9 8 7 6 5 4 3 2 1

First Edition

Printed and Bound in Hong Kong.

Distributed in the United States by Random House and in Canada by Random House of Canada Ltd.

A NOTE ON TRANSLITERATION

Bhutanese names are given in simple phonetic spelling, which gives only an approximation. Ph indicates an aspirated p, *which is the usual* p *sound in English. Tsh indicates an aspirated* ts *sound, as is heard, for example, in the word* invincible. *The few Sanskrit words current in popularly used names are given without diacritical marks.*

Library of Congress Cataloging-in-Publication Data

Markus-Gansser, Ursula, 1941–
  The dragon kingdom.

  Translation of: Bhutan.
  1. Bhutan—Description and travel. 2. Bhutan—Description and travel—Views. I. Olschak, Blanche Christine. II. Gansser, Augusto, 1910– III. Title.
DS491.5.M3613 1988   954.9′8   88-18221
ISBN 0-87773-454-2

Cliff Monasteries and Castles

Padmasambhava, called Guru Rinpoche, "Precious Teacher."

Curtains of mist, now hanging like lace veils, now thickening into bizarre shapes, move over the primeval forests of the Bhutanese highlands. Still higher, about 800 meters above the Paro Valley in western Bhutan, a cliff monastery sits snugly among tufty Himalayan cedars on a precipitous cliff face. This is the monastery of Taktshang, the "Tiger's Nest." And indeed this wild region may well once have been their haunt before these mighty cats drew back before the onslaught of man into the impenetrable lowland jungles at the foot of the Himalayas.

Taktshang was founded in 747 C.E., when the Tibetan Buddhist missionary and peacemaker Padmasambhava passed through the "southern land of Mön" from east to west. The "Lotus-Born One" is venerated by the sect of the Ancient Ones, the Nyingmapa, as the second Buddha and is known as Guru Rinpoche, "Precious Teacher." Guru Rinpoche was accompanied on his campaign by his mystical consort Yeshe Tshogyal, the Tibetan "wisdom spirit," who founded a convent in the vicinity, on the other side of Paro. Through numerous renovations and expansions over the following centuries, the Tiger's Nest grew into an intricate complex; some of its individual buildings are connected only by steep ladderways. Above it, a newly built temple rises in which the four Guardians of the World keep watch.

From the heights of Taktshang, one looks down over the fertile rice fields in the plains of the Paro Valley. On the south bank of the river are the low buildings of the Kyichu Lhakang, which, with the Maitreya temple of Bumthang, is venerated as one of the oldest holy places in the land. Stupa-like chötens in the temple's court bear witness to its founding by Tibetan missionaries in the seventh century.

In local tradition, Guru Rinpoche is remembered also as the restorer of these monuments, which, in the most varied sizes, mark the course of his movement from east to west. Each chöten is itself a representation and symbol of the Buddhist macrocosm and microcosm, and at the same time a reliquary. Above its stupa-like base (earth) rises a rounded shape (water), followed by the stages of enlightenment (fire), covered by the protective umbrella shape of air. This is crowned by the symbol of sun and moon in one (ether or space), the most popular sign for the unity of opposites, which is to be found everywhere in Buddhism—in regard to day and night, man and woman, and so on—always multidimensional and on all levels, material as well as spiritual. The five elements (including mind and the power of thought), for example, actually represent states of matter: solid—earth; liquid—water; transformational—fire; gaseous—air; mental, in the sense of without form and structure—ether or space.

The Nyingmapa, the sect of the Ancient Ones, or Red Hats, were not the only Mahayana Buddhists who settled in the Paro Valley over the course of the centuries. Followers of the Shakya sect, for example, also settled there. At the beginning of the thirteenth century, the first Drukpa monks came, the followers of the "Thunder Dragon" sect, named after their home monastery in southern Tibet. This school, a branch of Mahayana Buddhism or the Great Vehicle, was later to provide the state religion of Bhutan. Its spiritual and temporal leader, who in the course of the religious wars of his time left southern Tibet, was Zhabdung I, also simply called Drukpa Rinpoche. In 1616, he came with his followers over the western passes into the Land of the Mön and became the theocratic founder and ruler of the state of Bhutan. In Tibetan Bhutan is called Druk Yül, Land of the Thunder Dragon, after the Drukpa sect. *Bhutan,* the name in international use today, came originally from the name used by travelers from northeast India, and means "land of the Bhutas" or "Bhutias." This name for the Himalayan tribes corresponds to the common Northwest Indian *bhota* or *bhotia.*

Zhabdung I (1594–1651) became a unifying and protecting figure of such stature that his death was kept secret for some years so that the protection of his name and authority could continue to be used. Under his leadership the famous Bhutanese dzongs, castles, were built; still today these structures are the spiritual and administrative centers of the seventeen districts. Each is built at the strategically most important point in a valley—like Paro Dzong, with its ramparts tapering upward and a temple tower in the middle visible from afar. In the west of the Paro Valley is

Buddhist triad with the mystical Buddha Amitabha in the center, flanked by the four-armed bodhisattva Avalokiteshvara and Guru Rinpoche.

6

Zhabdung's "Dragon Castle," Drukgyal Dzong, today a burned-out ruin, which once secured the country against intrusion over the passes from Tibet.

The architecture always fits into the given topographical conditions, without violating Mother Earth—which would be tantamount to a desecration. Paro Dzong is a massive presence in the valley; Wangdiphodang Dzong rises by stages out of the crags; Punakha Dzong, the former royal winter residence at the confluence of the Pho Chu and Mo Chu (the "Father" and "Mother" rivers), is a castle with a moat. Part of the security system of most of the castles were watchtowers on nearby heights. These are in some cases still preserved. The present-day Bhutanese national museum, with its rich collection of Bhutanese art, is located in the large restored round tower above Paro Dzong.

During the regime of Zhabdung, who is venerated as a warrior and conqueror, a saint and reformer, and a builder of castles and temples, a unique event took place. Two Portuguese priests succeeded in reaching the presence of the theocratic ruler. They were greeted and honored as "lamas from the West" and were given their own small chapel. Their attempts at conversion, however, remained without result.

Already then, the Land of the Thunder Dragon, guarded by awesome gigantic mountains, was considered a mysterious and inaccessible country. However, from time immemorial caravan routes have connected Bhutan with surrounding countries. Thus there was a route from Tibet through the Chumbi Valley to Paro and from there to the Indian markets, where wares of the north—salt, yak-tail whisks, musk—were sold or exchanged for precious stones. Via a southward-running branch of the well-known "Amber Route," trade in this "golden gem" also reached Bhutan. J. P. Tavernier, who made six journeys to the Far East between 1631 and 1668, met Armenian merchants in the Patna bazaar who had introduced amber from Danzig into Bhutan and who reported the disappointment of the Bhutanese ruler when he learned that it was impossible to obtain an immense block of amber for a large Buddha image.

7

Page 9, left: Especially in the summer monsoon season after the frequent heavy downpours, thick clouds and fog banks pass over the forests high on the mountain slopes.

Page 9, right: Through a tapestry of branches and foliage, the Taktshang ("Tiger's Nest") monastery is seen. This monastery, high above the Paro Valley, was founded around 800 C.E.

Pages 10–11: Not far from Tiger's Nest monastery, set into the nearly perpendicular rockface next to a little windblown waterfall, is a hermitage, a place of strict solitary meditation.

Page 11: Here east of Lunana, in mountain fastnesses still hardly accessible today, ancient, continually renewed suspension bridges made of vines and bamboo connect mountain-slope settlements separated by torrential rivers.

Page 12, left: Wangdiphodang Dzong, built in 1639, a mighty fortress presiding over the confluence of the Sankosh and the Tang Chu.

Page 12, right: The moated castle Punakha Dzong was built in 1636–37 at the confluence of the Mother and Father rivers—the Mo Chu and the Pho Chu. This renowned fortress served the ancient kings as winter residence and was thus often regarded as the capital.

Page 13: Characteristic of the landscape of Bhutan are the rice fields in the plains of the high-elevation river valleys—here in the valley of the Paro with its dzong of the same name, built in 1646, in the background. Rice thrives in Bhutan up to an altitude of 2500 meters. Painstakingly cultivated, it has been the wealth of the country for centuries. The astonishing fertility of many highland regions, with their man-high stands of Himalayan rhubarb and "radishes" the size of children's heads, is probably due to subterranean volcanic activity, which also manifests itself in hot springs.

Pages 14–15: Another natural and much-used resource of Bhutan is bamboo, which is to be found, along with alpine conifers, up to considerable altitudes. With a short dagger or with the Bhutanese sword, it can be fashioned into the finest wovenwork and into long, stable suspension bridges. The swaying footbridges are laterally fortified with bamboo mats, but are nevertheless crossed at respectful intervals.

Page 16: Bhutanese mothers often carry their little ones secured with woven straps on their backs. A bunch of leaves serves as a sunshade for the child. The hair of the women is cut as short as that of the men, and on their shoulders gleam silver brooches, which hold together their uncut wraparound dresses.

Page 17: To winnow grain, the women use flat, loosely woven bamboo bowls, while the men bring them the massive sheaves.

Page 18: In an airy corn-storage loft made of bamboo mats, two Bhutanese women strip corn from the cobs. For protection against the sun they wear the round, flat bamboo hats common in the south.

Page 19: In Laya at the foot of the legendary Masang Kang at an altitude of about 3800 meters, the women wear heavy water-repellent coats woven of sheep's, goat's, and yak's wool and with a typical stripe-and-cross pattern. That they wear the pointed cone-shaped bamboo hats called mönpa *in spite of the penetrating cold of the high mountains could indicate that they come originally from a more southerly region of the country.*

Page 20: Children in the market street of Thimphu, the Bhutanese capital. The girl at the right stands under a wheel of dharma.

The Land of Mahayana Buddhism

In the midst of the capital city Thimphu rises a great, brilliant white chöten, built in honor of the king Jigme Dorje Wangchuk (1952–1972), the father of modern Bhutan. The interior has been covered by monks with religious paintings. On one wall is the portrait of a monk that was photographed for this volume while being painted (p. 37). The figure with hand raised in the gesture of debating is the Indian master of dialectic Dignaga, a highly inspired teacher who propagated the Mahayana teachings in the fifth century C.E. He is one of the famous eight sages known as "the two greats and the six jewels [of wisdom]." These sages appear in religious paintings in frescoes and thangkas (classical scroll paintings) as spiritual fathers of Mahayana Buddhism. In the usual iconographical composition, they flank the central figure of Shakyamuni Buddha, the founder of the Buddhist teaching, either singly or in pairs. One of the two "greats" is Nagarjuna, the primary guru of Mahayana Buddhism. Nagarjuna is said to have rediscovered holy scriptures containing Buddha's words in the realm of the nagas. The nagas appear in mythology both as dragonlike serpents who dwell in the depths of the sea and as "dragon men," shy inhabitants of the lowland jungles who wear snake skin on head, neck, and shoulders. Nagarjuna is also said to have received the sacred scripture on *Transcendental Wisdom* from a naga princess.

According to the Tibetan tradition, Nagarjuna was born four hundred years after the Buddha's Parinirvana (486 B.C.E.) and lived to an extremely advanced age. This master of yoga is said to have been the abbot of the great Buddhist monastic university, Nalanda, in central India. At Nalanda his teaching was further developed by his student Aryadeva, who is usually represented as the second of the "greats." Nagarjuna taught the practice of the six virtues, which is connected with a complete understanding of the relativity of all forms of existence.

One of the "six jewels," Asanga, who lived in the fifth century C.E., especially stressed the importance of yoga, in which mental and physical forces are "yoked" together. He also often appears with Nagarjuna as one of the "greats." Asanga's

Nagarjuna *Aryadeva* *Asanga* *Vasubandhu*

successor as abbot of Nalanda was his younger brother Vasubandhu, whose most important student is said to have been Dignaga. The latter taught in particular the unity of opposites, that inseparability of the absolute and relative truths that is expressed in a simpler form in all symbolic pairs. Day and night, sun and moon, man and woman (in the well-known embrace of the yab-yum, or father-mother, posture), bell and scepter—these belong together. And all aspects of existence are impermanent, empty of absolute eternality.

Dignaga's main student was Dharmakirti, who was succeeded by the leading sages Gunaprabha and Shakyaprabha, two distinguished teachers who taught concern for the well-being and good of the many. These ideas are a central element in the teaching of the Great Vehicle, Mahayana Buddhism, which shows the path to

Dignaga   *Dharmakirti*   *Gunaprabha*   *Shakyaprabha*

all people through the guidance of the bodhisattvas, or beings of the enlightened level. These beings enter voluntarily into rebirth in order to show suffering-ridden humanity the path to nirvana, the final salvation. Only by following their guidance is it possible to free oneself from karma, the ineluctable process of cause and effect through which, as a result of our deeds, we repeatedly experience rebirth in the maelstrom of the wheel of life.

Since the annexation of Tibet by China, Bhutan is the only country in the world in which Mahayana Buddhism is the state religion. In confrontation with the demands of the modern world, this tolerant philosophy has clearly shown its adaptability. The ancient traditional principles and knowledge are being newly formulated in simple form and understandable language and published by the traditional blockprint method. These principles are more urgent recommendations than binding commandments—guidance on how one may avoid harm and accumulate good deeds—for only the sum of past and present mental and physical actions determines one's destiny.

Sixteen general rules, the "virtues," promote well-being:

1. Trust in the Buddha, the religious law, and the religious community.
2. Rectify the three human faculties—thinking, speaking, acting; that is, put them in harmony with religion.
3. Respect your parents.
4. Show respect for all who are more experienced, older, and wiser than yourself.
5. Bow before all who are older and spiritually accomplished.
6. Be honest and decent toward friends and relatives.
7. Let your lifestyle benefit your countrymen.
8. Look up to those who set a good example.
9. Use food and possessions with thrift and prudence.
10. Return good for good.
11. Never cheat with weights and measures.
12. Be just to everyone.
13. Never envy others.
14. Never heed evil insinuations.
15. Speak politely, clearly, and kindly.
16. Always be generous, tolerant, and patient.

These ancient precepts for relating with one's fellows are to be found in a Bhutanese blockprint dated 1965. Possibly this time-honored folk wisdom is one of the causes for the cheerfulness and serenity that are reflected in the faces of most Bhutanese and that are the ultimate goal of all striving in Buddhism.

The extent to which the Buddhist path is a path of images is shown by the sym-

Protective, power-conferring mantras in mandala form around a mystical buddha in yab-yum (father-mother posture) with his mystical consort.

bolic representations of religiophilosophic principles that one plainly encounters every time one visits a temple. Frequently—as, for example, in the main temple of Paro Dzong—gigantic frescoes flank a temple entrance (endpapers, Picture 1). In them the so-called Cosmic Mandala is gleamingly depicted, recalling for modern foreign visitors an artist's conception of the structure of an atom, with its nucleus and orbiting particles. In the center of vast, still-empty space, the spiral of the first movement forms, and multiple rings prefigure the formation of future elements. Out of this whirling movement arises primordial matter. Depicted on a two-dimensionalsurface, this mandala is nonetheless to be conceived of as multidimensional. Particular colors and forms stand for the different states of matter. Yellow and square or cubic forms stand for solid matter; white or light blue and round forms for water; flaming, flickering forms and the color red for fire; green for air. The whole is formed out of the blue ether of formless space. All of this corresponds to the microcosmic and macrocosmic conception that is reflected in the structure of the stupa-chöten (p. 7ff). It is the graphic depiction of primeval becoming, which leads to existence and then to passing away. Here is depicted only one of the countless world systems arising in endless space.

"The lamas must be mad!" was the desperate commentary of early Western translators, who were still caught up in their egocentric worldview. However, today many people—often in fact scientifically trained people—find that this strange primordial image communicates something significant to them concerning their own knowledge. Just what the basis of this striking coincidence is can only be suggested, for here we are dealing with ancient texts and concepts that were transmitted only orally for centuries and first committed to writing by one of the eight sages, Vasubandhu, in his Abhidharma writings. Later, after the spread of Buddhism in the Himalayan countries, these were translated word for word into Tibetan. Also in the *Heart Sutra* and the *Diamond Sutra,* which are part of the *Transcendental Wisdom (Prajnaparamita)* literature, every chapter calls attention to the impermanence of all existence and also—doubtless by way of analogical reasoning—describes the most infinitesimal particle of matter possible, invisible to the eye, around the nucleus of which other particles orbit. . . . Voices of meditative wisdom, transmitted unchanged from long ago, yet today surprisingly modern.

Less enigmatic, in fact very graphic indeed, is the other representation that is frequently encountered at the entrance to a temple. This is the well-known Wheel of Life, which depicts the path of sentient beings in the grips of their destinies, which is the fruit of their own actions. In the center appears a serpent, a red cock, and a black pig, the symbols of hatred, greed, and ignorance (in the sense of intentionally not wanting to know). These three poisons are what it is most important to avoid. This clear warning could be enough by itself to make one take the just

A depiction of the mystical power of the phurba or ceremonial dagger, which casts out all evil and symbolically pins it fast.

path and be born in one of the better realms—those of men, titans, or gods; for the evil forces of hatred, greed, and ignorance lead inevitably to the realms of animals, monsters, or to the hells. In the hells the old god of death, Yama, adopted from Hinduism, reigns, not as a Judge but as the conqueror of death, who without evaluating weighs the black and the white deeds against each other, meting out the destiny one has created for oneself.

These images are a warning to everyone not to enter the temple of Buddha heedlessly, but first to bring to mind the impermanence of all existence and to recognize that one is responsible for one's own destiny; and also that—thanks to an inherent divine spark (or whatever expression one wishes to use for this manifestation of grace)—through one's own willpower one can influence the result by redeeming black deeds with good ones. And because this divine spark—"potential nirvana"—is within every man or woman, it is considered good fortune to be born a human being. That this latent force, often repressed and hidden away, can be made to shine through through one's own effort is the true message of Buddhism. This is a message that is meant for all and everyone.

Another symbol to be found in the large entry halls of temples is that of the Thousand Buddhas, who appear in a thousand ages, ever ready to proclaim again the same great truth in words suited to the times. Their messengers are their "spiritual sons," the bodhisattvas, enlightened beings of the celestial sphere, depicted with celestial ornaments, who in their earthy incarnations work for the welfare of humankind.

Since all the Buddhist sects are in agreement as to basic religiophilosophical values, today there is scarcely any conflict among the various schools, though in earlier times these schools often fought each other bloodily. Many paths leading to the same goal correspond to many different manifestations of human nature. Ever again a great lama-guru arises who recalls this truth and smooths over the humanly understandable conflicts among the schools and sets them again on the good path leading to the goal.

Page 29: The large number of young novices bears witness to the vitality of the monastic tradition in Bhutan.

Page 30: In ceremonies of prayer and offering in the temples, the observer is impressed by the great monastic trumpets (left, in the temple of Bumthang) and by long rows of butter lamps on the alters (right, in the temple of Paro Dzong).

Page 31: A lama in Paro Dzong reads the sacred writings, which lie before him in the characteristic oblong format. His ritual implements are bell and scepter, one of the most popular symbols for the unity of opposites, one of the principal goals of Buddhist thought. Here the scepter lies on the little table, in front of the pitcher of consecrated water.

Page 32, left: Monks sometimes wear long goatees, like the one Zhabdung I, the theocratic founder of Bhutan, might well have possessed. He was known widely in his younger years as "Bluebeard" and later as "Whitebeard."

Page 32, right: Among the important monastic utensils is the portable censer of bronze or gilded silver.

Page 33: This lama of the Nyingmapa sect wears the traditional yak-hair wig in emulation of the miracle-worker Thangtong Gyalpo (1385–1464), who was the first to construct bridges made with iron chains in Tibet and Bhutan.

Pages 34–35: Silversmithing is one of the traditional Bhutanese artistic crafts. Bhutan is known all over the region for its beautiful jewelry and excellent swords.

Page 36, left: The national costume of the Bhutanese is made of colorful cloth into which stripes are woven. The cloth is woven from wool, imported cotton, or raw silk produced in the southeast of the country. In addition to striped patterns, Bhutanese women also weave flower motifs into the cloth.

Page 36, right: Embroidery and appliqué are men's work.

Page 37: A monk working on a fresco in the chöten built in honor of King Jigme Dorje Wangchuk in Thimphu. Here he is sketching the figure of the dialectician Dignaga, who taught in the fifth century. Dignaga is being drawn making the gesture of debate, symbolized by the raised hand.

Pages 38–39: For the painting of thankas or banners, the cloth—usually linen, more rarely silk—is stretched in a wooden frame and primed. Then the basic pattern is set out with light lines. In this picture it is a mandala framed by lotus petals on top of a double vajra, or crossed-thunderbolt symbol. Requiring long and painstaking work, these banners are still crafted from natural pigments, though natural materials are more and more being superseded by synthetic ones.

Page 40: Printing of prayer flags often takes place on monastery balconies. The carved wooden printing block is inked with felt rollers, the flag cloth is laid on it and pressed against it with another roller. Already the prayer flag is ready to spread its good wishes to all winds!

At the Feet of
Snowcapped Giants

Like many others, creation myths of the Tibeto-Burmese language family, which includes Bhutanese, are in uncanny accord with events known from the study of historical geology. They also in no way conflict with scientific theories concerning the origin of the universe. Thus it is told that at the beginning the land was covered with water for countless millions of years (other sources mention figures with fifty-one zeros). This corresponds strikingly with the Mediterranean Sea of ancient earth, named after the Greek goddess Tethys, the consort of Okeanos. This is the ocean out of which, in the Tertiary, rose great folded mountains like the Alps and the Himalayas.

In Tibetan myths, which we know only from brief citations, it is recounted that the waters drew back, leaving behind only the renowned turquoise lakes as a reminder. Among these are the Yamdog Tsho south of Lhasa and Sky Lake, Nam Tsho or Tengri Nor, north of the Tibetan capital. Moreover, the north-drifting plate of the Indian subcontinent continues to force the Himalayan range higher, about one centimeter per year. Thus it is completely within the realm of the possible that climatic changes caused by this relatively abrupt upheaval are reflected in the sometimes astonishingly precise descriptions of the ancient legends.

Topographically, only a narrow strip of Bhutan, along the southern border with India, lies in the region of the Terai, or lowland, which is less than 200 meters above sea level. In this tropically lush area, especially in the west, are tea plantations. In the east, where the mighty Manas flows into the Brahmaputra, is primeval forest; this still largely untouched region is a destination for elephant-back safaris.

The mighty mountains of the eastern Himalayan chain rise abruptly out of this narrow strip of Terai. In the days when the country was accessible only on foot or on horseback, the journey from the border station of Puntsholing to the capital Thimphu, over steep unforgiving mountain paths, used to last eight days. Today the journey on the winding, newly built road requires hardly a day. In the north, the continental divide forms the border with Tibet; only in the northeast does the valley of the Manas and its tributaries extend into Tibetan territory. Among the 7000-meter-high snowcapped giants in northwestern Bhutan, only a few footpaths, so-called "one-man passes," lead over the border. From time immemorial the most important caravan route to Central Asia was the route over the Lotus Pass, the Peme La, on the western border, which led from the upper reaches of the Tibetan Chumbi valley via Paro to India.

The mountains on the northern border form not only a political, but also a climatic, border, which separates the dry, rocky Tibetan highland in the rain shadow of the mountains of the "southern paradise," from the "land of sandalwood forests and precious medicinal herbs" (both names for Bhutan in old sources). The monsoon rains of May to September are the cause of Bhutan's fertility. Rice thrives to an altitude of 2500 meters, and bamboo with conifers and rhododendron grow to high enough elevations almost to touch the downswooping tongues of the glaciers. The region of high mountains in Bhutan extends over 250 kilometers from Chomolhari in the west past Kula Gangri to Garula Kang in the east. The snowcapped peaks, over 7000 meters high, bear for the most part poetic names, some with mythological significance.

The "White Glacier of the Three Spiritual Brothers" is the 7500-meter-high Kangkar Pünsum; the brothers are the indigenous Mönpa, the Bhutanese, and the Tibetans. Here is the source of the mighty Mangde Chu, which flows through central Bhutan from north to south and which joins the Manas near the border. Masang Kang, 7200 meters high, rises on the northwest border; it bears the proud name of one of the original Tibetan peoples. Also, from the time of animistic beliefs, the mountain itself has been regarded as one of the fathers of the tribe, a snowcapped giant keeping watch over his progeny, the Laya folk, who dwell at his feet.

At 7320 meters, Chomolhari (or Chomo Lhari) is the highest peak on the western border. It is actually called Jo-mo lHa-ri, "Great Lady of the Divine Mountain." She also is regarded in folk belief, even today, as a living being. This belief is

Woodblock for a Buddhist banner. In the center is the windhorse with the auspicious wish-fulfilling jewel, surrounded by animals symbolizing the four world-quarters—the garuda bird with a snake in its beak in the west, the dragon in the east, the snow lion in the north, and the tiger in the south. Between them are the eight auspicious symbols (clockwise from above tiger): lotus blossom, fish, parasol, Buddhist victory banner, the vase with the water of life, the conch, the wheel of the teaching, and the knot of meditation. The text consists of auspicious formulas.

43

not only supported by tradition but also by modern mountain-climbing incidents. The Lady of the Divine Mountain is the only one of the great snowcapped peaks of Bhutan ever to be climbed; all the other seats of the gods are still "virgin." In 1937 a climbing team with F. Spencer-Chapman and Psang Dawa Lama climbed the summit of the border mountain via the south-southwest face. The climbers barely escaped catastrophe and the descent took place amid fits of bad weather. Despite warnings by Tibetans and Bhutanese about offending the "goddess," in 1970 an Indian-Bhutanese team climbed the sacred mountain. They did, however, carry with them, to pacify the goddess, a consecrated Buddha image. The sacred peak was successfully reached. The Bhutanese member of the party, however, stayed back 100 meters and waited for his companions—he could not bring himself to tread upon the goddess with his feet. Nevertheless, the goddess sought revenge; a second group of climbers, which followed the first, never came back.

The Swiss geographer Augusto Gansser explored the northern high peaks along the Tibetan border with five geological expeditions over a period from 1963 to 1977. According to him, Bhutan is topographically divided into the already mentioned Terai strips, out of which the foothills of the Himalayas rise abruptly, reaching 4000 meters in places. Covered on the south side by tropical virgin forest, they are only sparsely settled. Toward the north they merge into the central highland. In this region, 1500 to 3000 meters in altitude, lives the majority of the population. North of the central highlands, the altitude climbs once again. On southern slopes the forests of conifers mixed with bamboo give way just at 4000 meters to juniper. On the northern slopes they peter out lower down into rhododendron thickets. Thereafter comes alpine grassland, the domain of the yaks. The snow line lies on the average at 5000 meters, with tongues of glacier reaching down to 4200 meters.

This stupendous landscape, which is already impressive enough at lower altitudes, charms through its juxtaposition of alpine and subtropical, even tropical vegetation. Among bamboos, powerful Himalayan cedars stand; from their

44

The thirty-five buddhas who forgive transgressions. In the middle is Shakyamuni Buddha, flanked by his two closest students.

branches luminous orchids hang down. In spring, magnolias blossom in the still-bare mixed forest. In Punakha, at an altitude of 1300 meters, citrus fruits thrive, and in the Paro Valley the rice fields on the terraced hills go up to an altitude of 2500 meters. In the east the lacquer sumac grows, and silk culture has been carried on for centuries. The success of this is evidenced by wonderful wovenwork of indigenous raw silk.

In the journal *Die Alpen* ("The Alps"), Augusto Gansser briefly described his experiences in the remotest mountain valleys of northern Bhutan, which he is one of the few Europeans to have traveled and explored. We shall cite here an excerpt concerning the highland district of Lunana, in the two principal valleys of which the source branches of the storied Pho Chu (Father River) spring. The district can be reached only by passes more than 5000 meters high. If these are snowed in, Lunana is totally cut off from the outside world.

Because of seclusion amid the snowclad mountains, old legends have been preserved in the traditions of the sparse population. These legends, transmitted only orally, continue to exercise a marked influence on the lives of these farmers and yak herders who must struggle continuously against great hardship. My two companions in East Lunana, otherwise so talkative, suddenly went dumb as we approached the south wall of the 7100-meter-high Zongophu Kang. Between the upper moraine and the cliff face, there lay a deep, dark blue lake. Above in the gloomy mist, wild hanging glaciers could be made out. The oppressive silence was only broken now and again by tumbling rocks or the uncanny thunder of an ice slide in the steep surrounding glaciers. Through the mirror-smooth surface of the lake one could see the moraine abruptly disappearing in the depths. In the cliff face behind the lake, there was a dark cave. However, because of the fearful gestures of my companions, I had to give up having a look. In truth, some foreboding seemed to weigh on this place. High up in the crags, one could hear a ghostly music that recalled the singing of sand-laden desert winds on rock walls. . . .

The tantric protective deity Vajrapani in his wrathful manifestation as bearer of the thunderbolt. He wears a tiger-skin loincloth.

In the evening in camp, gradually the talk came around to the strange lake:

One of the seven evil spirits of Lunana lives there. A long time ago, after they had been subdued in Tibet, these seven spirits wandered over the glacier into the remote valleys of Lunana. The most powerful of them are Parep and Nidupgeltsen, who live in the thin juniper forest near Choso Dzong, the most remote of Bhutan's dzongs. The spirits like these mountain forests, and woe to him who fells a tree in one of them! The evil spirits are also held responsible for the catastrophic floods that come about through sudden overflow of glacier lakes. The mountains of the Lunana group are dominated by 7200-meter Teri Kang in the west. Here in the western valley of the Pho Chu thirty years ago, a glacier lake suddenly overflowed. The flood wave, caused by ice fall from a glacier above, destroyed the moraine dam and the flood washed away bridges in the valley far below, as well as part of the Punakha Dzong. . . .

Not the least of benefits from geological research in this high-mountain region will be the ability to recognize the causes of such catastrophes early on and to prevent them through taking appropriate measures at the right time.

Page 49, left: Chöten Kora, located in eastern Bhutan north of Tashigang, is the biggest stupa in the country. On the square, stepped base, which symbolizes the earth, rises a large spherical form associated with water. This is topped by the levels of enlightenment, connected with fire. Above these is an umbrella shape, symbolizing air, and on top of that the symbol of the sun and moon in one, representing ether or space. This monument of the microcosm and macrocosm, which can be seen, shining white, from a distance, contains consecrated relics and sacred scrolls. According to local legend, Padmasambhava had the first of these sacred monuments built on his missionary journey in 747 C.E., and they still mark his path from east to west.

Page 49, right: As already in the time of the Lotus-Born One, camping in the inhospitable mountain forests, here at the foot of 7000-meter Kang Cheda, is a laborious undertaking.

Page 50: In majestic solitude, the snow-capped peaks on the northern border keep watch, as here in the Lunana Valley of eastern Bhutan, where the Pho Chu has its source. Characteristic of the small chötens of

Bhutan is a square, stele-like form. The ones shown here belong to the country's highest and most secluded temple fortress, Choso Dzong.

Page 51: At the foot of Chomolhari, the "Lady of the Divine Mountain," the ruin of a fortified tower bears witness to the struggle against invaders from Tibet.

Page 52: Heavily loaded yaks—domesticated specimens of this impressive breed of highland ox—move alongside a sapphire-blue glacier lake toward the 5300-meter high Gophu La, the pass between Lunana and Bumthang.

Page 53: An old Bhutanese from Thanza in the Lunana district, the most highly elevated populated area in the country.

Pages 54–55: The wonders of the Bhutanese mountain highlands have as yet been witnessed by very few. Here hoarfrost works its sorcery on rhododendron plants and lies like moss on rocks and heaps of mani stones, out of which poke branches with frozen prayer flags. The saussurea flower (below left) protects itself at an altitude of 4500 meters with downy winter fur.

Page 56: The northern border of Bhutan runs along the continental divide created by these snowcapped giants. The easternmost and least well known of these Himalayan peaks is 6500-meter Garula Kang. Here the mountain forests with their Himalayan cedars grow up to 4100 meters, while tongues of glacier plunge down into thick rhododendron jungle.

Page 57, left: The rough peaks of the Tsenda-Kang group are reflected in a lake covered by a thin layer of ice in the 5000-meter-high Wagye La, a pass leading to Tibet.

Page 57, right: The first snow lies on the sparse meadowland around a still lake in the region of the Zakar Pass in northeast Bhutan.

Pages 58 and 59: View of the north side of the approximately 7000-meter-high Tsenda-Kang group, the most savage, and still scarcely explored, mountain chain of northern Bhutan. Left in the picture is the snow-covered main peak.

Page 60: This sapphire-blue lake in the granite mountains of the northern Lunana district is fearfully avoided by natives, since it is thought to be inhabited by an evil spirit.

The Magic of Dance in Bhutan

As once in Tibet, it is still traditional in all lamaistic monasteries of Ladakh—and here and there also in Sikkim—to put on magnificent mystery plays. However, nowhere is the magic of dance and of the dance drama so impressive as in Bhutan. Here the dances not only are preserved in an extraordinarily pure state, but also are a part of the life of the people. According to local legends and old blockprints not yet known in the West, Padmasambhava in his manifestation as Guru Rinpoche is the founder of these masked mystery dances, to which, in Bhutan, fascinating lay dances with a sense of the archaic can be added. The biggest festival of the year is the birthday of Guru Rinpoche, the date of which is determined by the lunar calendar and comes at the end of March or in April. In Paro it is celebrated with mystery plays and warrior dances in the great square, below a gigantic thangka hung on the temple wall.

Uddiyana, located on the Swat River in present-day Pakistan, was the mystical homeland of the great tantric masters and miracle-workers. From here came Padmasambhava, the Lotus-Born One, who won great renown in Tibet as Pemajungne. He was the great teacher who was able to tame hostile spiritual forces and bind them to the service of the new religion. He bound local demons and fierce gods by oath, forcing them henceforth to serve only Buddhism. This power of the Lotus-Born One, described in countless legends, can also be understood as a wise approach to religious politics, whereby forms of deities familiar to the shamanistic Bön belief system were preserved for the people. This made the old gods' new function as protectors of the good even more precious. Their fierce appearance and frightful weapons, now symbolically wielded in the struggle against evil, seemed almost calming.

This battle on a gigantic scale to subdue the demons and transform them into protective deities is celebrated in the ritual masked dances. These are rites in which the primeval magic of dance and of the art of maskmaking were placed in the service of the new religion so as to set before the eyes of the marveling people the spectacle of the struggle against evil and the victory of the good. The Lotus-Born One, who made the old serve the new in so many ways, was subsequently to be venerated as a second Buddha, and called Guru Rinpoche, "Precious Teacher." It is by this name that he is known in Bhutan, through which he journeyed from west to east in about the year 800 C.E. In the east of the Land of the Mön, as Bhutan was then known, in Bumthang, bards now recount this journey in a vividly ornamented fashion that is connected with the tradition of ritual dance.

The story is told of a dramatic encounter between Guru Rinpoche and the still-hostile old gods. To overcome them by guile, the demon-queller put on a fabulous masked dance play, in which he himself appeared in his eight manifestations and in eight dances brought to bear the entire force of his magical art of transformation. All the hostile gods rushed to the scene, even the highest of them. However, White-Gleaming Crystal Skeleton appeared at this time in the form of a lion. Guru Rinpoche was aware of the peril, knowing that this god had stolen the life-force of Sindhu Raja. He changed himself into the primordial bird Khyung (Garuda) and approached, beak and claws at the ready. In a dance of flight, he stooped upon the hostile demon, sunk his claws in the lion's neck, and seized possession of the sick king's life-breath and blood spirit.

In these traditions, two levels of consciousness and spiritual perception are always fused together. On one side, there is the religiosymbolic content; on the other side there is the manifested form, the legendary story that is acted out in the masked dance. Each onlooker can understand the event according to his level of consciousness—as abstract and symbolic, as a story, or simply as "real." Everything is present in these traditions—all possibilities and meanings on all levels. The confrontation described above presents only one interpretation, which accounts for the ritual dances in Bumthang as a struggle against the demons.

Exactly as the demons were converted, so were the oldest pre-Buddhist traditions of dance and maskmaking placed in the service of the new religion. These

*The bodhisattva of compassion, Avalo-
kiteshvara, in his four-armed form holding
a lotus blossom and a rosary, flanked by
Manjushri and Vajrapani. This is a Buddhist triad symbolizing compassion in its
connection with wisdom and power.*

were, so to speak, straightforwardly and openly brought in through the front door, so that they would not in later generations, because once pitilessly repressed, vengefully push their way back in through the back door, no longer susceptible of being developed into a controlling force. And thus a formerly murderous horde of demonic figures became servants of a peaceful religion and revel now behind masks in the drama of the play, in the turbulence of the dance, in ritual steps taken to the rhythm of instruments. Today, where every foreigner and many a native sees the reality of a historical moment, for the initiated observer there is only the symbolic act of transmuting—but by no means repressing—all the poisons that menace the process of spiritual liberation.

The dance dramas of the great monasteries, found in all of Bhutan's seventeen districts, have already become a tourist attraction in the western part of the country and are also performed for guests at other times than on the appropriate holidays. To the Western eye, they are a baffling, magnificent show.

The art of dance, however, is not only taught in monasteries for the mystery plays. Particularly in Bhutan, folk dance is also a great tradition. By the wish of the king, it is supported by the state, so that it can be preserved even in a capital now opened to the achievements of the twentieth century. Bhutanese men dance with unparalleled vigor, always accompanied by their magnificent singing. They practice in the villages and in the district centers, the dzongs, under the strict tutelage of a dance master, who for major performances also takes on the role of choreographer.

We were able to observe the activities of such a dancing school on the castle grounds in Tongsa. The dance master stood in the middle, beating time with a whipstock. The men, dressed on this occassion in their short-hemmed everyday clothing, circled around him. Every barefoot step, every movement, was sure, complete, and polished. Crosswise stamping steps became thunderbolts, which symbolically trampled all evil into the ground. This movement is related to steps in the ritual dances. Now followed a round dance, which developed intricate figure-eights that dissolved again. This was the warrior's dance that is performed by

Power-generating protective formulas in a round mandala form with the eight auspicious symbols. Folded small and tied with string, they can be carried on one's person or worn in an amulet.

laymen in warrior's armor on Guru Rinpoche's birthday to usher in the mystery plays. The whirling high point of the warrior's round dance is the archaic sword dance, usually performed by village headmen. It begins with an ancient war cry and continues with classical movements of the sword—whetting, wielding, striking—that make the blood rush with their magic. This dance can also be interpreted in two ways. Once it was a real expression of martial prowess; today it is a vivid spiritual display in which the sword cuts through nothing more nor less than the clouds of ignorance.

Another old custom in which the lay art of dancing shows itself with particular beauty is one that will soon also be lost in Bhutan. This is the custom of "dancing in guests." We were able to experience this in Tongsa Dzong in all its charm and enchantment. The visitors' caravan from Castle Altan rides over steep mountain paths with steps carved in the rock. As soon as it is spied approaching the Dzong, the long monastery trumpets intone a greeting. The guests dismount in front of the castle gate and are received by the welcome dancers. They are without masks, but decked out in colorful, swaying headdresses and the customary dance costumes of varicolored striped silk. As the line of visitors enters, they dance before it the whole way, symbolically but unambiguously cleansing the guests of all evil. With every step they trample evil into the ground; with each movement of the dance and with the sound of bells and small drums they shoo away demons that might be harmful to the visitors. Dancing in this way, they go briskly forward, through all the courtyards of the castle and out through the gate, over the bridge all the way to the door of the guesthouse. Hardly has the visitor entered his quarters before he can admire from his window a round dance of farewell, which is meant to ensure his well-being, free from all evil influences.

The different population groups, and above all the different sects and their monasteries, all have their ways of celebrating New Year with masked dance dramas, similar in substance but differing in details. This festival is celebrated according to the lunar calendar on the first new moon of the new year—according to our calen-

A mandala of sacred letters in a circle of thunderbolts, or vajras.

dar, usually the beginning or the end of February. Also the anniversary of the foundation of a monastery or the birthday of the founder of a sect are occasions for celebration, as is the arrival of an important guest.

For each festival particular dance dramas are chosen. In principle all of them proclaim the triumph of good over evil, though with countless variations. Mixed in are the charnel-ground or skeleton dances with death masks. These dances warn of the impermanence of all that is animate and admonish us to accumulate as many good deeds as possible, so that we can open for ourselves the way to a better future life and to the final release from the wheel of forced rebirths. This is also the principal theme of the death dance, which can still be seen, for example, at the Swan Temple northwest of Bumthang in its original form.

Page 69: In Bhutan, as in all of Central Asia, a bronze brazier with wood or yak dung is the only source of warmth. If the fuel is a bit too moist, the chimneyless room quickly fills with acrid smoke, which escapes only slowly through the bow windows, which are boarded up in winter.

Pages 70–71: In Monggar Dzong, the district center east of Bumthang built around 1930 in the traditional style, temple dances take place in the large forecourt. The monastic orchestra, with its large standing drums, long horns, flutes, and cymbals, sits on a mat, while two lay musicians beat the gong and the jungle drum. Barefoot dancers, all men, wear masks and colorful fluttering skirts and swing smaller versions of the standing drums.

Page 72: The foundation of Ngang Lhakang, the Swan Temple in the west of Bumthang, is commemorated with a festival in which the main lama rides around the temple on a white horse, led and ceremonially received by local dignitaries, who wear long white scarves over their shoulders. Pilgrims from the entire region flock to monastic festivals to attend the mystery plays and dances.

Page 73: At the anniversary of the founding of the Swan Temple, a lay dancer appears, making mighty leaps in the air.

Page 74: Tongsa Dzong, the first massive buildings of which were built in 1648, is the castle seat of the kings of Bhutan. The picture shows the staircase entry to the west wing, a later addition, with its richly ornamented doors, windows, balconies, and galleries.

Page 75: Protective deity in a dance drama at Tongsa Dzong. Five death heads crown the grimacing half-animal, half-human mask with its great fangs. Despite its terrifying appearance, it has a calming effect on onlookers, since it directs its wrath only against enemies of the religious teaching.

Page 76: Bhutanese musical instruments. The simple conch-shell trumpet, the rightwise-spiraling shell of a sea snail (above left), like the thighbone trumpet (above right) is used only on certain ritual occasions. The large conch trumpet encased in gilded silver (below right) sounds shrill and loud like a call to eternal life, while dancers wearing crowns

adorned with peacock feathers swing small double drums (below left).

Page 77: Along with monastic dance, lay dancing, supported by the state, is of major importance. Here the dancer portrays a warrior, fully armed and wearing a round head ring.

Page 78: The old demons and gods with their gruesome faces, which were taken over by Buddhism from animistic tradition and transformed into protective deities, always appear in the mystery plays. The picture shows two masks differing only slightly from each other in detail.

Page 79: Two particularly fine specimens of death-head masks from the charnel-ground dances, which recall the impermanence of life and the fact of rebirth. The red-clawed skeleton hands seem to call upon us to perform good deeds.

Page 80: In the monastery courtyard in the capital Thimphu, lay dancers demonstrate their stupendous leaping ability. Wearing colorful skirts gathered to the knee, they leap into the air from a standing position and double their bodies to such an extent that their heads sometimes touch their feet.

The Coronation of the Youngest King in the World

In July 1972, immediately after the death of his father, the Bhutanese king Jigme Dorje Wangchuk, Jigme Singye, the Fearless Lion, was confirmed as his successor on the dragon throne in a modest ceremony in the palace garden of Thimphu Dzong. The second, nonpublic coronation ceremony then took place at the former winter residence, Punakha Dzong. In this ceremony the principal lama of the Bhutanese Drukpa sect blessed the young king with the five-colored royal scarf, the rainbow colors of which symbolize the five wisdoms, the quintessence of all of existence. The date for the third, public coronation was painstakingly determined according to astrological aspects, and fell out, of all times, in the monsoon season, at the beginning of June 1974. For foreign guests of honor, fazed by the prospect of fog, downpour, and ceremonial processessions beneath umbrellas, this was rather intimidating timing. Their fears were, however, largely dismissed by the Bhutanese, who dignified them only with an enigmatic smile. They had confidence in their "weather lamas," who through their magical powers would chase away the rain spirits at the appropriate time. And—almost unbelievably for foreigners—that is exactly what happened.

Promptly on the first day of the coronation, all the clouds disappeared, and during all the days of the festival, a warm sun shone from an unblemished sky. The people, in holiday clothing especially made for the occasion, streamed in from all parts of the country. Guests were put up for the occasion in newly built Bhutanese-style houses. With the ceremonial procession of lamas, who marched by with the victory banners of Buddhism and other auspicious symbols, all the magic of ancient tradition unfolded, as well as again with the lay dances and mystery plays.

This occasion also showed the ability of the Bhutanese to combine new and old in a harmonious and pragmatic way. The guest houses built for the coronation ceremony were so planned and equipped that they could later be used in the state-fostered development of tourism.

Page 83: On the first day of the coronation ceremonies for the lion king Jigme Singye, born in 1955, the ceremonial procession of lamas with victory banners and auspicious symbols moves with measured step from the royal palace to the castle of the capital Thimphu. The four auspicious days for the ceremony were determined astrologically, and in spite of the monsoon season the finest of summer weather prevailed.

Page 84, left: On the roof of Thimphu Dzong, Drukpa monks salute the approaching procession of lamas with long horns, flutes, and cylindrical banners, the victory standards of Buddhism.

Page 84, right: Adorned with leaf-wreath headdresses, the staff of the royal household marches to the coronation square.

Page 85: The band of the royal guard strikes up for the festival in its traditional uniform with ear-flap helmets but with modern clarinets.

Page 86: Drukpa monks in festival vestments and with their characteristic hats bear the auspicious symbols in ceremonial procession into the monastery courtyard, where the novices sit expectantly in a semicircle.

Page 87, left: The family of the young king sits at tables of honor: in the turquoise-colored blouse, the Queen Mother Kelzang; on her left, her mother and the second widow of the royal grandfather; on her right, the two sisters of Jigme Singye, Sönam and Kelzang, and a step-uncle.

Page 87, right: King Jigme Singye, the Fearless Lion, on the dragon throne during the coronation ceremony on June 2, 1974.

Page 88: The radiant Queen Mother Kelzang with her daughters Sönam—the older of the two princesses—on the right and Kelzang on the left. Both daughters hold coordinating positions in the government. The Queen Mother's heavy necklace is of turquoise, which is said to bring good fortune; coral; and legendary zhi stones, or banded agate, which are highly prized throughout Central Asia and are traditionally bequeathed to the eldest daughter.

Page 89: After countless ceremonies the king enjoys himself at archery.

Page 90. One of the high points in religious ceremonies in Bhutan: the giant appliqué thangka with the likeness of Padmasambhava or Guru Rinpoche, "Precious Teacher," is unfurled on the wall of the temple. This particular thangka was made by monks over a number of years especially for the coronation ceremony, in order to place this ceremonial act under the protection of the great Northwest Indian missionary and to recall his journey through Bhutan, the Land of the Mön.

Bhutan Between Yesterday and Tomorrow

The theocratic rulership of Zhabdung I (1594–1651 C.E.) was inherited according to this ruler's wishes by his reincarnations, in whom, however, spiritual and temporal power was no longer united. The spiritual leadership fell to the dharma raja, the temporal to the deb raja. From 1616 until the end of the nineteenth century Bhutan was able to protect its independence successfully, apart from occasional, always repulsed, incursions from the north and skirmishes on the southern border that occasionally escalated. Between the visit in 1626 of two Portuguese missionaries and 1921, only twelve diplomatic missions, all British, succeeded in visiting the Bhutanese capital.

Beginning with G. Bogle, who arrived in 1774, all visitors were greatly impressed by Bhutanese hospitality. Only the military expedition of R. B. Pemberton, which was to explore the routes of the eastern Himalayas, ended unsatisfactorily but nevertheless—entirely in accordance with the intentions of the diplomatic Bhutanese—peacefully. Coming uninvited, Pemberton found neither guides nor provisions. He was, of course, not hindered; however, only the most difficult paths and routes were shown to him, so that the expedition had to turn back, exhausted by endless false marches.

At the end of the nineteenth century, according to the chronicles, reincarnations of Zhabdung I ceased to be produced, and the strongest of the lords of dzongs and district princes, Urgyen Wangchuk of Tongsa Dzong, seized power. He was recognized and supported by the people and thus became the founder of the present dynasty. A born diplomat and politician with astonishing foresight, he allied himself with the British, the then dominant colonial power in Asia.

As advisor to the British expedition that penetrated via Sikkim to the Tibetan capital of Lhasa, he was able to forestall the outbreak of further hostilities and was later knighted by the British for this. He was a close friend of Sir Charles White, the British representative in Sikkim, who lived in Gangtok. In 1902 Sir Urgyen Wangchuk invited White to Bhutan. During his third visit to the Land of the

Thunder Dragon in 1907, White took part in the formal coronation of the Bhutanese leader. In 1907 White was instrumental in concluding the treaty by which the British, with the proviso of mutual consultation in foreign affairs, recognized the independence of Bhutan and—a rare thing in its Asian diplomacy—gave up establishing a diplomatic post there. The diplomatic seat remained in Gangtok and the representative of the British crown could visit Bhutan only on invitation. (When India became independent in 1949, the big southern neighbor succeeded the British as party to this treaty.)

King Urgyen died in 1926; his son and successor Jigme reigned until 1952. Jigme's son, Jigme Dorje Wangchuk, was to become, in the twenty years of his reign, the father of modern Bhutan. After a lucky escape from an assassination attempt, in 1967 he took over the leadership of the government and opened the country to modern times by giving it a new form of government, which is still in force today. Thus Bhutan is a constitutional, hereditary monarchy, with seventeen districts and a national assembly, the Tshongdu. Of the Tshongdu's 150 members, 100 are elected from electoral districts, 10 seats are held by lamas and 40 by high officials appointed by the king. The business of government is directed by a ministerial council and a royal staff of advisors. This organization ensures that the ancient social structure of the Bhutias, based either on clans or villages, will continue to exist.

In 1968 King Jigme Dorje gave up his right of veto; in 1969 he made it constitutional for a king acting against the welfare of the people to be deposed. In May 1972, perhaps having a premonition of his imminent death, he officially installed Jigme Singye, born in 1955, as crown prince. After his death in July of the same year, as the people mourned, Jigme Dorje's body was ceremonially cremated in the Temple of the Future Buddha in Bumthang.

So it is that in seventeen districts, each with its dzong as religious and administrative center, a Himalayan people lives, whose 1.2 million people speak fifteen different languages or dialects, preserved in the remote mountain valleys. Six of these

Auspicious mantras with the double thunderbolt, or vajra. In the middle is placed the sacred letter HUM, so that divine blessings may be actualized on earth.

dialects belong to the *dzongkha* or official dzong languages and are taught in all the mandatory schools. In addition English and Hindi are compulsory subjects.

Today roads through the passes make Bhutan accessible from the south and west. They are the most visible result of the five-year plans subsidized by India. Since 1983 Dragon Airlines has connected Bhutan with Calcutta (the direct flight is canceled often during the summer monsoons). Since 1962 Bhutan has been a member of the Columbo Plan, since 1971 of the United Nations, and since 1983 of UNESCO. The Bank of Bhutan was founded in 1968, and in 1969 Bhutan became part of the world postal organization.

Though tough and true in conserving the old, the Bhutanese nevertheless keep their eyes open and can quickly adapt what is useful to them. An example is aid for development. When China occupied Tibet and hermetically sealed its border with Bhutan, important traditional pasture lands were lost. Bhutanese herdsmen then began to burn down home forests in order to increase their pasture area. This is a process which, as the Nepalese example shows, produces ominous results when carried out on a large scale. But, quietly, help was on the way. F. and M. Schulthess, Swiss friends of the king who recognized the danger in time and were familiar with Swiss alpine land management, privately began initial land-and-forest-management projects to show how forests could be kept and livestock yield increased at the same time. The first project was launched in 1967 in 3000-meter-high Gogona. Today the Bhutanese themselves are continuing it. Later the "Pro Bhutan" foundation was founded. As its tasks and responsibilities increased, administration of the Bhutanese projects was taken over by "Helvetas," the Swiss economic aid and development organization. The young king and all Bhutanese are working today to follow the lead of the late king in combining what is good in their tradition with what is beneficial in modern ways.

Page 95: The Temple of Maitreya, consecrated to the Buddha of the Future, in the valley of Bumthang. Next to the Kyichu Lhakang in Paro, it is considered the oldest Buddhist temple in the southeastern Himalayan region and is thought to have been founded by Tibetan monks in the seventh century C.E. Possibly originally only a small sacred site marked with chötens, in the course of the centuries it developed into the most favored site for cremations. For in wood-rich Bhutan, the open-air burials of Tibet, in which corpses are exposed to the vultures, are not customary. Here corpses are burned in a formal ceremony. The rectangular so-called cremation chöten is made of light bamboo mats. Poles with prayer flags edge the cremation place, where crows await the remains of the funeral meal that follows the burning.

Pages 96–97: Pictures of the cremation ceremony. Each sect has set up its own tent. The tents are set in the four cardinal directions. The monks are playing long horns and trumpets, chanting texts from the Book of the Dead, preparing food offerings, and holding bundles of kusha grass in readiness for the ceremony. On a day determined by astrological calculations, the cremation chöten with the corpse arranged in a crouching posture inside it is burned (far right). The yellow cloth on the bamboo wall bears the inscription "Urgyen Rinpoche" (Padmasambhava).

Pages 98–99: Many people have come from a great distance to take part in the cremation ceremonies; the occasion is the cremation of a high lama who had predicted his death as well as indicated the time and place for the burning. And exactly as predicted, a rainbow circle appeared around the sun and then it rained for days without stopping. After the cremation, all the guests are invited to the funeral meal.

Pages 100–101: Scenes that are still rarely photographed. After the cremation, the ashes of the high lama are strewn in the river or are mixed with clay and formed into small chötenlike cones, tza-tza, which are also cast on the waters or preserved as relics on the shrines of consecrated chötens.

Page 102: A monk holds a small bronze skull used in tantric rites and dances as a ritual vessel.

Bhutan

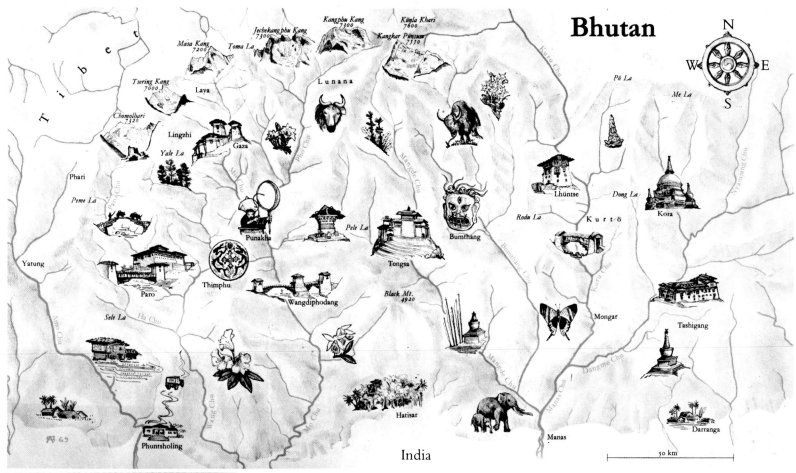

Bhutan or Druk Yül, the "land of the Thunder Dragon," is a constitutional monarchy with approximately 1.2 million inhabitants. The state religion is Mahayana Buddhism of the Drukpa Kagyü school. Dzonkha, the "castle language," a dialect of the Tibeto-Burmese language family, is the official and school language. The currency unit is the *nu (ngultrum)*. One nu equals one Indian rupee. The country, 46,600 square kilometers in area, borders in the north on Tibet and in the west, south, and east on India.

SOURCES OF ILLUSTRATIONS

AUGUSTO GANSSER: *pages 9 left, 11, 13 right, 17 right, 40–60, as well as the back of the dust jacket and the map sketch, p. 103. Francesca Gansser: page 74. All other photos are by Ursula Markus-Gansser.*

TEXT ILLUSTRATIONS: *Calligraphy on p. 2 by Tshenshab Rinpoche. All other illustrations are reproductions from woodblock prints on plant-fibre paper, as produced by the woodblock-printing process in Himalayan monasteries. The iconographical representations of the eight sages of Mahayana Buddhism are from* rGyan-Drug-mChog-gNyis *(Gangtok, Sikkim: Institute of Tibetology, 1962).*

ENDPAPERS: *The frescoes reproduced here show the origin of our universe—one of countless world systems. Picture one (inside front cover) is the Cosmic Mandala of the "beginning," resulting from the first movement in empty space, still free from form and structure. The spiral in the middle—a primeval form of the swastika of the first movement— is to be seen as multidimensional. It is surrounded by the turbulent rings of movement of the primordial elements, symbolized by rainbow colors (see pp. 24–25).*

PICTURE TWO *(facing picture one): Cubes and squares (represented in two-dimensional form, where spatial depth is absent, as squares and circles) show the further development of materialization. From the center of the mandala, surrounded by birds and clouds, the Tree of Heaven symbolically grows.*

PICTURE THREE *(facing page i): The silhouette of a monk is seen in the entrance to the temple of Bjakar Dzong in Bumthang, built in 1676. The capitals of the upward-tapering wood pillars are painted with rows of lotus blossoms in luminous rainbow colors. In this form they adorn all such half-timbered temple structures, which are constructed without the use of a single nail.*

PICTURE FOUR *(facing page 104): Precious appliqué thangka portraying one of the four Guardians of the World. Characteristic are the magnificent headdress and the large rings in the earlobes.*

PICTURE FIVE *(facing inside back cover): Here the tree takes on more definite form. It bears the symbols of celestial worlds and is flanked by cloud-scraping mountain summits reaching into the heights. Brooks flow and the first plants are sprouting.*

PICTURE SIX *(inside back cover): In this mandala the forms are already fixed in the classical pictorial style of Buddhist cosmography. Forms and colors symbolize the different elements or states of matter. Thus yellow and cubic or square forms signify solid matter—earth. White or light blue, flowing or rounded forms correspond to water. Red and flaming, flickering forms stand for fire. This representation of perpetual origination, existence, and passing away is rendered in a pictorial language based on long-forgotten texts, which in its fixed formalism is no longer clearly understood.*

BIBLIOGRAPHIC NOTE *For comprehensive bibliographical information, see Blanche C. Olschak,* Ancient Bhutan: A Study on Early Buddhism in the Himalayas, *limited English edition with large maps, published by the Swiss Foundation for Alpine Research, Zurich, 1979. Augusto Gansser, "Der Bhutan-Himalaya," in* Die Alpen 2 *(Bern, 1983), and* Geology of the Bhutan Himalaya, Denkschriften der Schweizerischen Naturforschenden Gesellschaft, *vol. 96, Basel, 1983.*